SEE THINK FEEL ACT:
500 Prompts Toward Disruptive Success

Gordon F. Holbein, Ph.D.

SEE THINK FEEL ACT:
500 Prompts Toward Disruptive Success

Copyright © 2017 by Gordon F. Holbein
All rights reserved.

ISBN-13: 978-1544074054
ISBN-10: 1544074050

CONTENTS

Inspiration & Premises 1

Setting A Stage 3

Opening Minds? 5

Funny Things About Thinking 15

Do Opposites Dance? 35

Standing Apart, Standing Out 41

What Matters Most? Less? Not Much? 47

Sitting Naked Spitting? 53

The Whole Purpose 61

The Fine Art Of Results 67

Our Influence With Others 79

Life's Greatest Opportunity 99

The Spirit Within 113

Onward 115

INSPIRATION & PREMISES

"Every science begins as philosophy and ends as art." (Will Durant)

"Imagination is more important than knowledge." (Albert Einstein)

"We don't see things as they are. We see them as we are." (Anais Nin)

"When 'everyone knows' something … nobody knows nothin'." (Andy Grove)

"You can't do what everyone else does and expect different results." (H. Lee Scott)

"No problem can be solved from the same level of consciousness that created it." (Albert Einstein)

Inspiration & Premises

"The opposite of one profound truth may very well be another profound truth." (Niels Bohr)

"The test of a first-rate intelligence is the ability to hold two opposed ideas in the mind at the same time, and still retain the ability to function." (F. Scott Fitzgerald)

"There is nothing so practical as good theory." (Kurt Lewin)

"The real voyage of discovery consists not in seeking new landscapes, but in having new eyes." (Marcel Proust)

"Some ideas are so stupid that only an intellectual could believe them." (George Orwell)

"Still a man hears what he wants to hear, and disregards the rest." (Simon & Garfunkel)

SETTING A STAGE

I started formulating these thoughts when someone very powerful said to me, "Because I said so."

Thoughts came even faster when I was told, "Because that's our policy."

Other contributors include:
"Well obviously,"
"Go your own way" (Fleetwood Mac),
"That's just the way I am," and
"Live free or die" (New Hampshire).

Recently I started painting abstract impressions with oils. I am prolific. My most moving works emerge as I let go of the tendency to manipulate the outcome – and rather let the process flow as it may. So too here. So too in the most vital elements of life.

Setting A Stage

If you read my other two books, "The Tao Of Leading Effectively" and "500 CEOs: Lessons From The Heart," you will see the origins of the observations of this volume in the ancient philosophies of the East, and in the current applications of the West.

This book is incomplete. A new edition should be issued next month. Think.

The observations in here are imperfect. Argue with them – anything to examine our assumptions. Question.

OPENING MINDS?

Curiosity is delightful.

Take wonder in others.

Don't pretend to know everything. Don't know everything yet.

Be soft with your tone, but rock hard with your facts.

Be still. Listen. Peace, be still. Be still and know.

Let it be. Let it flow. Let it grow.

In order to act more effectively – see more clearly, think more broadly, feel more deeply, listen more care-fully.

Opening Minds?

Read the news, not because it matters directly in your life, but because it opens doors for you to become wiser and more interesting.

We want more and more of what we already know or believe. Democrats want more and more liberal talk. Republicans want more and more conservative talk. Believers hunger more and more for faith. Unbelievers hunger more and more for doubt.

The Greatest Challenge In Learning is carefully considering ideas that don't appeal to you, instead of turning away from them. Big enough?

None become great by isolating themselves from "unfairness" of a brutally competitive world. Retreating in fear? Working harder in faith?

Opening Minds?

Do you know anyone who doesn't run away from reading or listening to things that are contrary to what they like to believe? who does not become defensive, avoidant or hostile?

Glass is fragile because it's rigid. But plastic is resilient because it's flexible. To endure, learn to bend.

What are you curious about? What intrigues you? What fascinates you? What do you stand in awe of? Feed curiosity! Be useful and interesting.

Talk is cheap. Advice is cheaper; you get what you pay for. Opinions are the cheapest. Mere opinion is worth less. Every uneducated person on the street has an opinion. Every uneducated boor has an opinion. Nobody wants your advice, or mine either.

Opening Minds?

Choose to collaborate closely even with those who see things differently from you. Lead the way!

You will learn, grow and progress when you open yourself to ideas that are different from yours.

We are far too interested in things we already agree with.

A Powerful Force in our lives: Our disdain toward, and refusal to listen to and consider, words that are different from what we like to hear

Creativity, discovery, learning, innovation, change, growth, progress, success require tolerating and working with ideas contrary to yours.

School is about getting a job only to the degree that life is about work. Since life's more than work, your education should be very broad.

Opening Minds?

Everywhere you go, ask people what they have learned so far in life.

If we are not changing, we are not learning. You will never learn anything from those who simply agree with you.

The Most Valuable Advice differs from what you already think, believe, know, feel, and do. If not disruptive, how much added value is there?

Leadership 101: Can you bring together and harmonize the interests of people with very different priorities? Emphasize the big picture.

The more we learn about others who are quite different from us, the greater opportunity we have to learn about our own self. Branch out.

Opening Minds?

When someone gives you a gift, the point is not whether they got you just what you want or need. The key is for you to learn to appreciate it and them.

Wanted: Someone who is willing and able to get us to challenge our assumptions.

Wherever you go, be intrigued with people's life stories. Be hungry for insight. Invite their experiences to open your eyes, mind, heart.

If you do not believe that you are at least a little bit ignorant, naïve, or gullible, you are in trouble. #Hubris

Think of when a parent, teacher, friend, boss said you could act/do better. Did you react with defensiveness, or with gratitude?

Opening Minds?

The Fundamental Law Of The Safe, Sheltered And Small: Be sure to reject or tune out anything contrary to what you like to think.

Be very sure to not be completely sure of yourself.

Will your thinking and ideas become clearer and sharper if they are sheltered, or if they are examined and challenged?

If you agree with everything you read and hear, you aren't learning.

Step One: Learn to un-learn.

When someone says something that makes you uncomfortable, when do you consider that they actually may be making a good point?

Opening Minds?

The longer you win and win and win without a setback, the harder it becomes to learn.

You Should Read Books that you are not fully comfortable with. If you only read what's comforting, you are not challenged or growing.

In order to be clever you must listen closely to what others think and feel.

People Who I Have Trouble Trusting: Those who always have a convenient answer proving that they are never wrong.

Asking one more question is more valuable than knowing every answer.

To see more clearly, think more broadly, and feel more deeply, strive to listen more care-fully. Then we can act more effectively.

Opening Minds?

When all experts agree, head the other way; something else is going to happen. And the surer the certainty, the bigger the shock to come.

If you can't explain your point in simple terms, you haven't fully mastered it yet.

When a mangy, drooling, dangerous dog comes at you, don't run; that would imperil you and make things worse. So too with the words of radicals.

FUNNY THINGS ABOUT THINKING

Data can be found to support all sides.

Data are manufactured. If data are tortured, they will confess as you wish.

Faith is a choice. We either choose to have faith, or choose to not have faith.

The very act of believing creates what we see.

What we see is a reflection of what we are.

What we say we see in others is a projection of what we sense within our self.

Nature is a grand, wonderful wonder-filled teacher. Examine very small things.

Funny Things About Thinking

Beware of dangerous delusions such as: Because we have done it before, it makes sense for us to do it again. Because others do it, it makes sense for us to do it too. This time is different; the old rules no longer pertain. My little world is (or at least is reflective of) the universe.

Applause is the third most seductive narcotic.

There are three sides to every coin.

How many instruments, how many voices can you hear in the music? Listen carefully and deeply, focusing on the unnoticed sounds.

Science is merely one method for approaching some types of knowledge.

Our most significant knowledge comes not by science nor by calculation.

Funny Things About Thinking

Our most significant knowledge comes by sense, thought and revelation.

Virtually all that we do is based upon hope, belief and faith, not knowledge.

All purposeful action manifests faith.

Faith is a mental exertion, a choice put into action.

Faith well-placed is power.

Faith ill-placed is impotence, or demise.

When we say, "It's been proven that..." or "Everyone knows..." We often are (in reality) simply accepting what others have told us.

Watch your self thinking, and observe your feelings.

Funny Things About Thinking

All elite performance requires unique, undeviating, singular focus (within a fitting perspective first framed).

Most of our actions occur not as the result of decisions. Our most significant decisions come not by science nor by calculation. Decisions hinge ultimately upon belief, hope, faith, and trust. Our most significant decisions come by desire, hope, belief, faith, feelings, moods, emotions, intuition, needs, subjective perceptions, advice, interpersonal pressures, social expectations, and that which we do not see at present.

Most of us identify a person of common sense as one who sees as we do. So, what would be uncommon sense?

A fish knows water only after it leaps out.

Funny Things About Thinking

Seek some quiet. It is fertile ground. Listen. Reflect..

Do not flee from chaos, uncertainty, ambiguity, turbulence, change, dynamism, paradox or the like. These are fertile ground.

Averages have practically no reality, nor reality to individuals.

Regression lines are distracting fiction while outliers are fascinatingly instructive.

Every generation believes that its time is the most disruptive of all eras.

Every generation believes that the rising generation is lost, and the prior generation is clueless.

Funny Things About Thinking

What foolishness are we swallowing blindly today as being clearly "obvious"?

We learn not the lessons of the past but by living them.

Much of one's success hinges upon one's ability to sift through chaff to the kernel, fruit, germ, core.

All things pass.

Repeated interactions of randomness produce patterns of apparent order. We then lay our own logic upon this mystery. Thus, the appearance of order may be illusory, especially where human agency has a role. Yet we persist in fearing randomness as causation, and subject it to the hegemony of science.

Funny Things About Thinking

Recent trends will continue. Now is likely to be forever. Ha! In good and bad, don't ever fall for this.

Everything that every person does everywhere always makes complete sense – to them. At least, so they will tell us.

Understanding principles is greater than following rules.

Orientation is greater than a map.

78% of all statistics are made up (on the spot). Or, is it 87%... ?

Great Strategic Thinkers are first and foremost great readers and listeners – astute observers first.

Funny Things About Thinking

When confounded by vast complexity, turbulence, dynamic uncertainty, dilemmas, or paradoxically competing demands and predicaments, go way back down to foundational fundamentals: "Well, we do know this, and this, and this for sure."

Wait; pause. Be still; be quiet. Withhold a rush to speak, judge, solve or fix. Cut through the clutter. Quietly, clearly let the fog and mist dissipate.

Etymology prompts revelation.

Scientific facts and absolutes known to be true by everyone have never been actually observed by any but the few. (e.g., Water is H_2O; $E=mc^2$; the nature of gravity, etc.) Instead, they are accepted as articles of faith in the religion (hegemony) of science. And if their full proof were presented, it would be generally incomprehensible. Thus, we function very well (best!) as naïve true believers.

Funny Things About Thinking

You cannot prove that water is H_2O, yet we all enjoy the benefits of water. So too with air, sunlight, nutrition, DNA, digitization… All proof begins with faith.

It is much richer to be taught how to see than how to think, but that is much more useful than being taught how to act.

There is no good or bad art. Its goodness or badness resides only in the evaluator, not in the work itself.

Arts are of greatest worth when simply absorbed or experienced without interpretation, commentary or explanation. The interpretation of arts denies their soul and extinguishes their spirit.

Our greatest opportunity is to make positive choices about how we think and feel.

Funny Things About Thinking

Read the news only to search for themes, universals, and maybe trends.

Most of the news has little or no bearing on our daily conduct.

We all live by assuming that the future will look like the recent past.

All that seems so big now will pass away.

Today's worries will turn out much better than feared.

Invest more and more time bathing in, soaking in music, silence, sunshine, rain, art, nature.

To think better, first get quiet and still without and within.

Funny Things About Thinking

As we journey and mature, we come to focus on and appreciate the weaving more than the loom, the person more than the position, the method more than the money, belongingness more than bureaucracy, meditations more than machinery, hugging more than hurrying, praying more than possessing, music more than mathematics, singing more than statistics.

Imagine a competition where all people participated in a grand elimination bracket, as is often found in sporting leagues. After 33 rounds, one person is left with no losses – the champion. He or she would be deemed as the best. If the process in each round was stochastic (e.g., coin flipping), the results would still appear equivalent as if skill, reason or mechanics were involved. Thus, we may retrospectively impute skill, reason, or functional mechanics to that which may be more random than we want to see.

Funny Things About Thinking

Observe your thoughts. Manage them. Observe your feelings. Manage them.

We walk through our days viewing our interactions either through an adversarial lens (survival of the fittest), through a collaborative lens (symbiosis), or through a sacred sacrificial lens (love).

How you think is more significant than what you know. So education is more important than training.

What we believe or don't believe depends more on what we want to believe than on whether it is true or not.

Full Power requires that we be real about what causes what. Let's not fool ourselves.

Funny Things About Thinking

Negative thoughts and feelings may be "realistic," but reality can be changed by choosing to think and act positively.

Focus your mind and your will for a concentrated period of time, and you'll be amazed how much you can achieve above your norm.

Concerned about the future? Virtually no one sees the path ahead clearly. We all progress just one step at a time. Focus on right now.

Want to foresee your future, how far you will go, how high you will rise, how much you will contribute? Just look at the personal standards that you currently are living.

When we pay dearly for something, we then twist dearly to justify the cost.

Funny Things About Thinking

All Too Common: Determining what is right/wrong, good/bad based on whether you like it or not. Credible? Reliable?

Notice how people use the word "fair." Too often what we mean is "good for me," rather than... unbiased, even-handed, equitable, impartial.

Focus, and train the pattern of your thoughts. Mindfulness is much more than meditation.

We think great thoughts because we have read, listened to, and pondered great words, and because we have been through crucibles of experience.

I will have greater power and success as I focus my thoughts in spite of daily distractions.

Funny Things About Thinking

Focus; train your feelings. Emotional self-mastery is the first key to power.

Situations are not stressful on their own. Stress is a way we think about situations.

A strategic perspective enhances all our endeavors. So rather than judging or condemning what appears to be "absurd," dig deeper, be open.

Power comes in relentlessly focusing on what matters most.

Although all of human senses are susceptible to illusion, bias and confusion, it is miraculous how we progress. Have faith in life itself.

People are figuring out how to act by seeing what others are doing. Sometimes smart. Sometimes foolish. Always shortsighted. Lead the way!

Funny Things About Thinking

Decision-Making 101 Be very wary. We are able to find/create "evidence" that supports anything we want to believe or do. #ConfirmationBias Knowledge is fluid. Every time you step into it, it changes. (Ponder the Tao)

Those who call successful people "lucky" never seem to make much progress themselves. Just like those who frequently say, "I deserve."

Before making any decision, all of us should say, "I am biased, and I don't have all the facts."

The power of managing your thoughts/emotions is potent.

You don't need to be an optimist to focus on what is positive and good. You don't need to be an extrovert to be friendly and speak up.

Funny Things About Thinking

When we focus on thoughts of stress, we make short-sighted decisions. There is a peace within that is greater than our circumstances.

In the midst of chaos still your mind. Still your heart. Remember your ultimate purpose. Focus on your values. Act accordingly in faith.

The Most Significant & Powerful change you will ever make will be to adopt a new way of thinking.

Looking Backward: 75% useless, 20% harmful. Face forward, move on!

To start thinking, stop busying. Single silent solitude

Many of our biggest problems and most troubling challenges will shrink dramatically to the degree we are willing to change the way we think.

Funny Things About Thinking

Being alone with ideas is powerful, and dangerous

The Priorities Of One Destined To Not Lead & Not Contribute Much: My feelings. My needs. My desires. My image. My money. My security. My comfort. Let go of fear.

Most writing, and most speech have far too many words. Most listening has too little silence.

It is likely that we are either doing too much and reflecting too little, or reflecting too much and doing too little.

All humans need spells of unbroken quiet, solitude, peace in order to refresh and renew. The use of media is a counterfeit for this process.

Funny Things About Thinking

Be very hesitant to make anyone your hero or role model unless you have walked closely with them for many miles.

The old, familiar saying is, "What's the worst they can say, 'No.'?" The better way is, "If I don't ask, they have no chance to say, 'Yes!'"

Before you decide what to do, first consider how you can see more clearly, listen more care-fully, think more broadly, and feel more deeply.

Facing the facts in life. Beware of "Strategic Ignorance" – the tendency to avoid info that may disturb us.

Numbers don't lie? Perhaps. But keep in mind that numbers are simply shadows of what's really going on.

Funny Things About Thinking

On what basis do we believe and trust what we read and hear? If it fits with what we already feel sure of? By using self as our standard, what progress do we miss out on?

DO OPPOSITES DANCE?
DO OPPOSITES – DANCE!

All Of Existence – from the subatomic to the galactic, things material and immaterial – is made up of paired opposites. Balance & Wholeness

Within the maximum are the seeds of the opposite, the opposition.

The yin is not much without the yang, and the yang is dangerous without the yin.

The dynamic cycling of opposites gives rise to creation. Yin and Yang cycle counter-clockwise, the dynamic tension of their contraposition generating cycles of creative destruction. It is the dance of life.

Play with the opposite. Just consider it… Put it on the agenda.

Do Opposites Dance?

Do not ask, "Well, which is it, A or B?" Ask instead, "How is it both A and B?"

Become the thumbtack – broad and deep. Breadth is humanity. It facilitates touch, feel, discernment, and effectiveness. Broaden your horizons. Depth is focus. Deepen your expertise. It facilitates efficiency.

Small and simple things are the elements of greatness. They are the tools of the great ones.

Balance is founded upon center and ground.

Center stands with good clear values.

Ground is established in integrity. Integrity is wholeness.

Do Opposites Dance?

Chain(ed) restaurants put their least mature employees (in canned routines) first in the public eye, while fine establishments first present the public with the touch of well-aged maturity and refined sensibilities.

Nature is brutal and placid, harsh and soft, unyielding and adaptive.

That which is not whole cannot be eternal.

Neither the diverse elements, nor the unified field are sufficient in and of themselves.

Do less with more, thus resisting the rush to efficiency.

Scratch where there is no itch, and there soon will be one. So too with most annoyances.

Do Opposites Dance?

There is no need to respond to everything. But we should be responsive to everyone.

Hearing is related to volume in an inverse-U relationship. So too with understanding.

Most seeming di-lemmas are not mutually exclusive. See the sides as complementary.

Division creates; unity sustains.

Strategic Paradox: Diversity brings broad perspective while unity brings power and potency. Yin-Yang

It's likely that you're either taking too much risk, or not enough risk in your life. (And reflect: not acting can be very risky.)

Do Opposites Dance?

We are in the business of producing results. But the more we prioritize results over people, the sooner our results will diminish.

It seems that many of us are being either too hard or too easy on ourselves.

You are either trying too hard, or not hard enough.

What you know, feel and believe matters far less than what you do. But what you do rests on what you know, feel and believe.

Whatever you are experiencing today, it will change. If it's good, get prepared. If it's not, live in hope and faith.

Go the extra mile, but do not run faster or labor more than you have strength. The wise and effective Servant Leader lives in balance.

Do Opposites Dance?

Most of us are too fearful or too foolhardy.

A Great Truth in all things: We move through cycles. Down goes up. Up goes down. When you're up, get ready. When you're down, get ready!

Who earns the most? The math wizards? The socially skilled? Those who balance both sides. So get busy updating your skill set.

Those who demand simple, black-or-white, all-or-nothing answers have given up on thinking.

STANDING APART, STANDING OUT

What intrigues you? What are you fascinated with? What do you stand in awe of? So feed your curiosity. (If nothing especially comes to mind, you need to think about that...)

Creativity is seeing the same things as everyone else, but thinking something different.

To be outstanding, one must stand out.

To make a difference, one must be different.

To gain and sustain an advantage, one must be distinct from others.

Change is costly, risky and threatening – and vital.

Standing Apart, Standing Out

Play with the terrible two-year-old technique: Pursue linked chains of causal "Why?" "And why that?" "And why that?" On and on and on toward the root...

What will your grandchildren show you that will be incomprehensible to you in your latter years? Certainly not a mere extrapolation of what is cutting edge today.

The safest place to play is the middle of the road. Nobody drives there.

Ill-logic: "If everyone acted that way, things would fall apart."

No philosophy can stand up to itself. If so, it ultimately is mere tautology.

Standing Apart, Standing Out

If the fine print is so vital that it must be put on the screen, why is it unreadable?

Question implicate assumptions embedded beneath the complexity, turbulence, uncertainty, dilemma, paradox, competing demands, and predicaments. There will be found false, spurious, invalid, unfounded predicates distracting us from what matters most.

Frame-breaking occurs never for most, and once for the rest. Exceptions are exceptional.

In the Academy there are two professors. One is the Guardian, protecting the shrine of achievement and reward from the unworthy, unwashed masses. The other is the Facilitator, opening the gates and removing stumbling blocks to ensure that all who enter may see the mountain top.

Standing Apart, Standing Out

All this may, and should be, contra-dicted because exceptions are the rule.

I want all my students to earn an A. If they want to dither away the opportunity for education, that is fine. Get out of the way of nature's course. Karma, the Law of the Harvest, is perfect. What goes around comes around. We get just what we deserve.

The first social media technology was conversation.

Question assumptions. Examine the "obvious." Swallow nothing blindly. Become dangerous.

People who have had the greatest impact on the world were first thought to be crazy.

Whatever good/bad, strong/weak you see today will not continue forever. Change always comes.

Standing Apart, Standing Out

Creativity may be about technology, but innovation is about the customer.

There is no creativity nor innovation in isolation. We must interact with a wide variety of stories, people and ideas. Ignorant = out of touch.

To generate more creative ideas... 1. read more broadly, and 2. ponder quietly for longer.

When everyone believes something, when everyone loves something, when everyone says something, it's time to pause and think more deeply.

Stop saying: "Think outside the box." duh zzz... Anybody can say that (and everyone does). Instead, ask: "What box?"

Standing Apart, Standing Out

If everyone agrees with your ideas, you're not trying hard enough.

Be so good, so unique you are above and beyond others. At that point you're the one who sets the terms of engagement.

WHAT MATTERS MOST? LESS? NOT MUCH?

You are free to choose.

Don't get addicted.

Passion may be self-centered and blinding.

The pursuit of happiness as a purpose in life requires a fixed external standard so as to resist the risk of drifting toward self-centeredness and short-termism.

The whole nature of existence undisturbed is tending toward goodness.

Rank and weight your priorities.

Our real priorities are revealed in our actions.

What Matters Most?

Because every managerial act impacts other people's lives, every managerial decision calls for ethics.

Enduring, eternal truths and absolutes center and ground our understanding. Ask, "What absolutely matters most of all?"

All that we do reveals our priorities – what matters most to us.

Lack of clarity about our value system leads to shifting shiftlessness, dissipating our efforts and squandering resources. It is both inefficient and ineffective. This pertains to individuals and to organizations.

The vending machine at work is malfunctioning and dispensing snacks without requiring payment. Do you report it?

What Matters Most?

Clarity of one's value system produces focus. The integrity of acting accordingly leads to efficiency and effectiveness in optimizing efforts and resource utilization. This pertains to individuals and to organizations.

If you haven't clearly stated, and firmly committed to a set of ranked priorities, you are underperforming your potential.

Decide ahead of time what your priorities, values, standards are. Don't wait until the pressures of the moment are upon you. Lead the way!

People who highly prioritize having others praise and respect them find it very difficult to grow better and stronger.

Commit to what matters most. Sweep away what matters least. Priorities are power!

What Matters Most?

Those who truly desire to be more successful must first change their priorities. Or, they must act with more integrity to their theoretical values.

Are you able to adapt your actions without compromising your values? Knowing your ultimate purpose helps. Be strategic.

A strategic approach empowers all aspects of life. But that first requires determining what matters most, less, least, not at all.

If you change your standards in certain situations, then they aren't truly your standards.

If you discover that your actions do not match your beliefs/values, which do you change?

What Matters Most?

"So sorry I haven't gotten back to you sooner, but I've been really busy." Translation: "You're not that important to me."

A grand challenge in management and in all of life: Balancing competing priorities. How you cope with this defines you and your success. So, establish good, clear values.

If Friday is the best day of the week, and Monday the worst, are you on the right path? Start by defining what matters most to you.

Someone told me: "If I am happy, that means I am successful." Hmm, maybe so... But that can lead to short-termism and self-centeredness.

Before you "follow your passion" you must first establish priorities, master self-discipline, cultivate your curiosity, add value for others.

What Matters Most?

Is your work enacting what you value most in life?

SITTING NAKED SPITTING?

The purpose of business (and life) is to create distinctive value that can make others better off.

As we ensure the well-being and prosperity of others, we enrich ourselves.

The purpose of business is to harness random resources through the creation of value for others. The purpose of business is to organize and coordinate the application of resources toward value beyond what exists in their dormancy.

Business 101 Q: What is the proper price to put on a good? A: Whatever the public perceives to be the worth it brings to them.

First mover advantage is mostly illusory.

Sitting Naked Spitting?

Sustainable competitive advantage in cutting-edge domains is only had by patient opportunism, not by quick creativity.

Strategy 101: The leading cause of corporate failures is resistance to change. So too with individuals.

Is technological innovation proceeding exponentially? Will that continue? Will it accelerate? Can it? What is the asymptote?

Risk management is less than an oxymoron; it is a dangerous delusion. If it can be managed, it is not much of a risk.

Uncertainty is not risk. Uncertainty may lead to the perception of risk (i.e., the possibility of a negative outcome), but uncertainty just as likely can lead to positive and negative outcomes.

Sitting Naked Spitting?

Who defines "working" families, a "living" wage, and "fair" trade? Objective reality? Propaganda?

Business, when practiced ethically and legally, is one of the greatest goods for our world. And that can be a very noble profession. Without for-profit Capitalist corporations, families, government, schools, religious institutions, charities would have essentially nothing. If not for Capitalism, for-profit corporations, competitive markets, you wouldn't be doing anything today (except maybe scrounging around).

All ongoing business is socially beneficial. If we are not adding value to others and for others, we cease to exist.

Every material blessing that we enjoy and benefit from is the fruit of free-market Capitalism and for-profit corporations. Give thanks!

Sitting Naked Spitting?

If well-informed people voluntarily pay a lot for your services, you are not charging too much. You're delivering much value in their eyes.

Deceit corrupts the market's natural allocation of resources to their highest and best use by destroying participants' trust in transacted prices as valid and reliable signals of resources' real value.

Capitalism hinges upon morality (transparency and honesty without guile or coercion) so that well-informed buyers and sellers in free and efficient markets can act so as to allocate resources to their objective highest and best use.

Bribery is wrong because it shifts decision-making away from objectivity to non-value-adding considerations, thus corrupting the integrity (the efficiency and effectiveness) of rationally objective markets.

Sitting Naked Spitting?

The opacity of deceit is corruption.

If sellers and buyers cannot be well-informed, if transparency and honesty do not prevail, if there is guile, or if there is coercion, sellers and buyers cannot act rationally, and objectivity is lost, thus corrupting the efficiency and effectiveness of the invisible hand of supply and demand. Thus, markets fail and resources do not move to their objective highest and best use. This was in large part the core of the 2008 financial crisis, as multiple markets approached failure. In housing, commodities, equities, derivatives, labor, etc., market failure was manifest in the disconnect between market prices and inherent value. Deceit, misinformation, limited transparency, and manipulation were at the root.

Because there are not free and efficient markets for all things of value, morality must guide us.

Sitting Naked Spitting?

If D.C. mandated that we pay farmers more than what their produce is worth to us, would it be more nutritious? #MinimumWage?

Imagine: You and those in your city do business only with each other. Would you be wealthier? better jobs? more goods and services?

If your income is "too low," the market is telling you, "You are not generating sufficient unique value." True for firms and individuals.

Why are some rich, some poor? The Political Perspective: Because the "system" is rigged. The Economic Perspective: Because of their differing capabilities and choices.

Inequality of outcomes makes sense. Equal outcomes require us to see, feel, think, act, be the same. Only totalitarianism can enforce that.

Sitting Naked Spitting?

Those who cry "Abolish inequality!" will have their way when 1) we all think and feel alike, 2) we act the same, and 3) the "system" stops rewarding talent and effort differentially. Then there will be no inequality. Watch out!

A Fair Minimum Wage: The least someone is willing to be paid, assuming they understand all that's involved and are not coerced into it.

Adam Smith: "It is not from the benevolence of the butcher... that we can expect our dinner, but from their regard to their own interest."

If it were not for Capitalism and for-profit corporations, we would just be sitting naked in the dirt spitting.

THE WHOLE PURPOSE

Not making others better off makes one irrelevant. (Why would they need you?)

Add unique value to others' needs and wants.

Value exists in contributing toward real needs what does not exist otherwise.

A person who sucks the life out of life, and who adds little to the world, is one who focuses on how others impact them.

A person who adds life to life, and who contributes greatly to the world, is one who focuses on how he impacts others.

The question is not "What am I getting out of this?" but "What am I putting into this?"

The Whole Purpose

In a job interview, when the manager says, "Tell me about yourself," what they are asking is, "How will you contribute to our needs?" Prepare.

If people benefit from your work and pay for it, you're doing good for them. If a company has paying customers, it is doing good for society.

The more gratitude we feel, the more we want to help others. We've been given gifts for a purpose: making the world better. Lead the way!

Who has benefitted most from what you have done today?

Make your resume stand out from others: State your objective in terms of what you will contribute, not what you want to get.

The Whole Purpose

I just saw elevator repairman at work. I hope he didn't skip classes or cheat on his licensing exam.

A classic and enduring indicator of a successful life is one which adds value to others. Anyone and everyone can do this.

People who are concerned with getting the respect they feel that they "deserve" usually are not contributing much.

Self-Awareness: "I am who I am." Other-Awareness: "I understand why they are as they are." Value Creation: "I change my self accordingly."

You become valuable as you put yourself in other people's shoes and see how to make their lives better – true in business; true in life.

The Whole Purpose

The Fundamental Question Of Business: How can we add unique value in making people's lives better?

If you're working for somebody, either a boss or a client, you are there for one purpose: to make them better off. Focus on creating value.

All work can be approached as community service. The point is to create distinctive value for the sake of others.

To be wealthy, fulfill the needs of others in a distinctive way. To be a good person, fulfill the needs of others in a distinctive way.

There is no such thing as job security. The closest thing? An ability to understand others' priorities, and add unique value toward those.

The Whole Purpose

The best public speakers, the most successful salespeople, the bravest heroes, the greatest contributors – all focus on the needs of others.

To become more valuable to an employer and your clients, take responsibility for things that currently seem beyond your control.

The only way to create wealth is to increase one's productivity in doing things that others value highly. True for nations, firms, and you.

If you are not making others better off (employees, partners, customers, etc.), you are not going to be in business very long.

Two Choices Today – Attitude One: "What can I get?" Attitude Two: "What can I give?" Who will lead?

THE FINE ART OF RESULTS

Luck is not chance. Luck is of hard work and patient persistence.

All choices are what is wanted in that time and sphere.

We want to do everything that we choose to do.

We can't "work smarter" until we first work harder. Too many people talk like the two are unrelated.

More regrets come from acting sooner rather than later.

If a life's value is who we are, then truth, virtue, sacrifice and love are our ultimate priorities.

The Fine Art Of Results

Just as child's play is preparation for the adult world of work, so too is adult work a shadow of child's play.

As career guidance, passion is overrated. Try curiosity, or at very least passion as sacred sacrificial giving of self... not self-getting. That's what our grandparents did in the coal mines, in the dust bowl, in the slaughter yard or packing house, along the trail, on the docks or shop floor, and in the foundries.

That which is easiest to obtain is cheapest.

Bring passion into all the work you must do. Michelangelo didn't want to paint, but look at the Sistine Chapel!

Just face in the right direction, and take one more small step. It will come.

The Fine Art Of Results

First put words together with pencil on paper before committing to the computer.

Appearances matter if we assume that we learn best visually.

Everything has a cost. Whatever you get, you pay for.

How much do your happiness and success depend on who is President?

Belief without action is faithless. Life is far more interested in what you do than what you believe.

Nervous? Maybe even fearful? 1. Prepare more. 2. Care deeply about helping others. 3. Focus on a purpose bigger than the moment.

The Fine Art Of Results

Short-sighted: "Do what you love and you'll never work a day in your life." Work is wonderful, uplifting, ennobling! Work harder.

Communication Skills: No one writes well without revising, revising, revising. No one communicates well without much reading and listening.

Maturity 101: Learning to like that which is necessary, even if you don't enjoy it.

To know what you should do, determine who you should be. Success begins within.

We hear two things a lot: "Find success by following your passion." And, "Success is measured by whether you are happy." Self-centered?

If after all your very best effort, it doesn't work out – simply move on. Better things are out there.

The Fine Art Of Results

Our best, strongest, proudest, most noble moments: When we do what we really don't want to just because it's right and others count on us.

Complaining erodes faith and hope. But hard work optimizes faith, hope, change and success.

Stop thinking, "Follow Your Passion." Rather, chose to act passionate in whatever you are doing. Become powerful.

How you feel about your work (the world doesn't care) is far less important than how you act in your work.

In obtaining something, we give up another thing. Always.

The more you sacrifice and refuse to cut corners, the prouder you will be of yourself.

The Fine Art Of Results

The First Knowledge: Self-honesty. The Greatest Victory: Self-mastery Lead the way!

A successful student... acts with honesty and integrity, works hard, pursues curiosity, helps others, changes and grows. (And note, those things may, or may not, correlate with GPA.)

Every decision we make either broadens or limits our future opportunities. Who we are, and what we will be, is the sum of our choices.

When you find yourself saying, "I wish that... ," just work harder instead.

Want to see your future? Simply look at your choices today.

Cry Of The Shortsighted: "You're so lucky!" Cry Of The Distracted: "I deserve... !"

The Fine Art Of Results

How you feel is nice. How you act is significant.

It's Far More Powerful to act passionate about what you're doing now than to search hoping to find something that excites you.

Don't worry if you can't see your destination. You do see enough now to do what is good and right. And that will surely lead you to what's best.

Your circumstances affect you only to the degree that your decisions allow them to.

Choices are more important than circumstances.

Think of what would bring you great happiness. If you don't picture great cost, risk and sacrifice associated with that, you are merely dreaming.

The Fine Art Of Results

Genuine Self-esteem comes from making and acting on positive choices in the face of adversity, not from the praise of others (unstable).

Everything You Need to add value or degrade, be successful or fail, change or stay stuck, be happy or miserable is inside your mind and heart.

Don't Like Something? You have three choices: 1. Bear it. 2. Make things better. 3. Adapt, and change your self. But don't complain.

If you're consistently and persistently making good choices in the present, you surely will arrive at a good place in the end.

In education, investing, marriage, and in most of life, decisions that have the greatest impact are those made early on.

The Fine Art Of Results

I hope that we fail and fall short from time to time so that we learn to change, grow, improve and progress.

Every time you get something, you have given up something.

Our greatest hopes and dreams hinge upon our doing seemingly small and simple things today.

Your success is much more determined by your habits, character and personality than by your knowledge and skills.

Your power begins and ends with self-discipline.

Which matters most – what you believe, what you feel, or what you do? How would your boss, colleagues, clients want you to answer that?

The Fine Art Of Results

Your greatest opportunity in life is in closing the gap between what you know/believe and what you actually do.

The further you progress in your life's work, the less it should seem like a science and the more like a fine art.

A person is richer/poorer than others due to 1) circumstances, or 2) choices? Which one you feel is more significant foretells your future...

Even in boring meetings, clients colleagues bosses need and expect you be actively engaged and contributing. No excuses regardless. Prepare now.

Be clear regarding the difference between spending time versus investing your time.

The Fine Art Of Results

Framing wrongdoing as a societal problem distracts individuals from personal accountability and responsibility. So does calling it a "mistake."

If we were able to make everything go exactly the way we want it to, much of life's purpose would be voided.

Your most important work very rarely produces immediate, tangible benefit. Keep your focus on the long-term big picture. Patiently persist.

OUR INFLUENCE WITH OTHERS

While management is mostly science, and leadership is mostly art, managing strategically is a craft. It is best exemplified by Grandma in the kitchen. Just because Grandma is not reading a recipe, it does not mean that there are no rules and all is subjective opinion. She cannot substitute salt for sugar, baking powder for baking soda. Nor can she successfully bake at any temperature at random. Be like Grandma in the kitchen – crafting the way. It is a long process of learning by doing requiring intimacy and harmony with materials, high touch and high feel. The fundamental objective is clear. So, while abiding in true principles, she is both visionary and also teachable, incrementally adapting as it goes and grows. Sharing and passing it on, there is true joy in giving.

The more I teach, the less they learn that matters.

Our Influence With Others

Iron-Clad Law of Leadership: Before I can ever even expect to lead others, I must first learn to manage myself.

Founding Principle of Leadership Development: When I become the kind of human being I ought to be on the inside, then I may become the kind of leader I want to be on the outside.

Fundamental Question of Leadership: Am I becoming the kind of human being who others want to follow?

Leaders' true influence is born in virtue, love, and sacrifice — self-mastery, service, and work.

Remember to say, "I understand." And do not fear to say, "I don't understand."

Laugh. Laugh at your self and let others see this.

Our Influence With Others

People are hungry.

Because we are far from our eternal origin, we feel a hole in our hearts. We are unwhole here and now. It is a longing for home. We all are striving to fill that hole in our hearts.

Hungry hole-fillers may include: music, prayer, sex, God, chemicals, faith, food, sleep, applause, service, possessions, family, control, friends, exercise, sacrifice, anger, laughter, violence, repentance, intellect, virtue, money, nature, art, beauty, glamour, gurus, dreaming, risk-seeking, achievement, rebellion, change, tradition, power, competition, pity, blame, aggression, retreat, mantras, panaceas…

To effectively lead others, we must be able to see through their eyes.

Our Influence With Others

Make others look good in the eyes of those who matter most to them.

Get your eyes off the computer. Remove the earphones. Put away the phone. Disconnect the ball and chain.

When leaders try to explain their most strategic actions, they say, "We feel." To speak so with validity and genuine authority, one must be in touch. We cannot feel without touch. So, close the spreadsheets. Turn off the computer. Get out of the office. Go down to the shop floor. Get out in the field. Walk slowly through the crowd. Look them in the eye. Hear them breathe. See them sweat. Get in touch. Ask them, "Why? How? What?" Be one.

When one is stubborn, so too is the other.

Our Influence With Others

The worker's work is the task. The manager's work is the task through people. The leader's work is people in the context of a task. So because we are told to have passion for our work, leaders must care very deeply for their people. Love them above self. It is not about you.

Future generations will remember today's giants as legends, myths, or shadows, if at all.

Classics must be long old. Heroes ought to be dead.

Before you venerate another as an exemplar, let them be dead for a good while.

Heroes are those who willingly lay down their lives, or put themselves into harm's way, for the sake of others – especially without desire for praise or reward.

Our Influence With Others

The point was not what they could get to feed their passionate pleasures, but what they could give for others, for a higher purpose.

Loving sacrifice is a sacred sacrament.

Passion is sacred sacrificial struggle suffering overcoming. (Self-serving "passion" is a corrupt counterfeit.) Compassion is shared sacred sacrificial struggle suffering overcoming. Together they find pure religion.

Nobody will remember, and therefore benefit from, more than 100 words.

Exaggeration is enthusiasm's deceit. Everyone generalizes all the time.

All types of power are diminished by impurity.

Our Influence With Others

You will be a highly effective leader as you care about others, sacrifice, live with virtue, follow good clear values, and consider the big picture.

The greatest work of an executive is in shaping patterns founded in core beliefs, empowered in values, and expressed in norms. This provides the vision, mission, priorities, ethics, methods that give the organization life, humanity, focus and strength that are its vitality. It provides the center and ground without which it cannot balance through uncertainties.

You are influencing others. So now is the time to act equal to your full potential.

Leadership requires optimism.

Life rewards those who are positive, cheerful, friendly and other-centered.

Our Influence With Others

The primary role of all leaders is to help others. If they are not growing, you are not much of a leader.

If you say you have faith, you act on it. If you say you love, you act on it. Lead the way!

Why don't we have a Washington or Jefferson today? Sadly, we have divorced strong minds from strong spirit.

Stop and consider for a moment: That person who disappoints and/or frustrates you actually may be doing the very best they can.

Truly effective leaders desire to inspire the hearts of others, not just impress them.

Help others feel optimistic and confident. You are a leader.

Our Influence With Others

To have a fully developed sense of humor, to become more creative, to see further than most – first, laugh at yourself.

Truly good leaders see things through their people's eyes. This empowers both. Listen for understanding beyond just words.

When one finds themselves arguing, they are not showing leadership. Stop and look for a different path.

Anyone can be nice to those who are nice to them. big deal

To build a strong network, and a loyal following, incorporate some humor into your work no matter how serious.

Our Influence With Others

Hate is all around us. But so is love – the foundation of authentic and truly powerful leadership.

You are authorized to be cynical and to find fault only to the degree that you are sacrificing to make things better.

You can't whip people into shape. They must want it, or change will be fleeting. You will lose their heart. You, and they, will become less human.

Other people are counting on you to be positive even if you don't feel it. That is Emotional Maturity & Strength.

Two parties can engage via Capitulation (one gives in to the will of the other), via Compromise (both give a little, take a little), or via Collaboration (co-laboring in unity for a common value beyond self).

Our Influence With Others

Regardless, regardless, regardless of any type of differences among us – even very deep differences – compassion can be extended to anyone.

We all are both a student and a teacher every day of our lives.

Every person you work with has intrinsic worth just because they are a human being – regardless of their actions. You too. Bring that out.

Don't just look at others as they are now, but rather as they can become.

Nothing is ever gained by descending to the level of the rude, petty or ignorant. Lead forward and upward.

No act of kindness, no matter how small, is insignificant.

Our Influence With Others

True leaders care about others regardless of who they are. You need to lead.

Demeaning put downs are not leadership. Just the opposite. Leadership is building, not taking cheap shots. Create value.

Simply teach your people correct principles and allow them to govern themselves.

Stop. Before you ask a question, are you ready to deal with whatever the response may be? Too often we only want one certain answer.

Much or most of what we enjoy today was paid for by the sacrifices of those who came before us.

No one can be an effective leader without self-mastery / self-discipline. One of the most visible manifestations of that is in our words.

Our Influence With Others

The more you fight, the more you will be fought.

When you influence others, you are a leader.

What you say about others reveals more about yourself than it does about them.

Anger weakens our power to overcome. Anger erodes all power.

Too many words bring frustration.

Too many believe that leadership is only for those in positions of authority. But, whenever you interact w/ someone you can lift them up.

Virtue is power. And it makes life much less complicated.

Our Influence With Others

Ask leaders, "Do you care about the well-being of your people?" 99.9% say, "Yes!" Ask those people, "Do you feel well cared for?"

When others tell you something, quietly consider what is going on inside them. Effective leaders understand more than just words.

Walk above fear by focusing on love for others. A focus on self (needs, feelings, desires) amplifies fear.

Communication 101: If you don't explain why, people are likely to assume the worst.

Studies show that the more we go on and on explaining ourselves to others, the less credible they believe we are. Truth is simple.

How frequently you feel offended speaks volumes about the depth of your character.

Our Influence With Others

Everyone knows the power of good manners, polite behavior, and proper etiquette (everyone except a self-centered person).

Caring deeply for others is the beginning, middle, and end of truly powerful leadership.

Want to get somebody else to change? good luck with that.

Effective leaders require high standards while being mindful of human imperfection. Expecting more, they coach and mentor more.

Hungry for "everyone" to like you? Remember, even biggest show on TV (Super Bowl) attracts just 37% of the U.S. population. 63% have no interest.

You will be most respected when you cease to demand respect.

Our Influence With Others

Leaders are not born. Leaders are not made. True leaders choose to step up, to move forward, to add value, to serve, to show the way.

Beware of killing yourself by wanting, expecting, needing others to treat you in a certain way. Become whole. Move on.

Want to be powerful? to have great influence in the world? Cultivate genuine interest in others' lives, needs, preferences, experiences...

If you cannot (or will not) get others to do what they otherwise naturally would not do on their own, you will never succeed in management.

Before you ever think to correct another, they must first believe that you genuinely care about them, and that you see through their eyes.

Our Influence With Others

Beware the difference between striving to be likable versus striving to be liked. Develop a positive character, but do not give yourself up.

How many people do you know who are genuinely interested in others? in hearing what others think, do and feel more than telling their own story?

Want to have a great influence on others? Listen

If you don't prioritize listening to what truly matters in others' hearts and lives, you'll never really sell anything (especially not your self).

Anger and hatred are the poisons of self-centeredness.

Pure love focuses on the welfare of others. Its counterfeit, lust, focuses on self-benefit.

Our Influence With Others

Inasmuch as the work of leaders is their people, and inasmuch as we must love our work to succeed, then love is the heart of leadership.

The Leader With Emotional Maturity – acting not how you feel, but how you should. Dependable and worthy of our trust. Reliable. A rock.

Gracious leadership moves mountains. Show genuine interest in what matters to others. Serve their needs and wants. Say "thank you" often and sincerely.

Some of you may move the whole world. But each of us can in one moment, at one point, in one way touch one person. That will mean worlds to them.

Authentic leaders know this: "All my knowledge, talents, energy, gifts are for the purpose of uplifting and empowering the lives of others."

Our Influence With Others

In order to change someone's mind, we must speak in a way that can reach their heart.

LIFE'S GREATEST OPPORTUNITY

In order to move the world, we must touch individuals. In order to touch individuals, we must improve ourselves.

Many, many people have invested in you, and endowed you with gifts. It is your opportunity and responsibility to magnify those gifts by adding value to the world around you.

If you haven't failed at anything in the past 12 months, either you are way too timid, or you're fooling yourself.

We are bound by neither birth, nor by chemistry, structure, circumstance, experience nor heritage.

Inertia prevails and devolves.

Life's Greatest Opportunity

Moods and emotions flow naturally from our choices and actions. Moods and emotions should not drive our choices and actions. Act on correct principles, not moods or emotions. This is emotional maturity and strength.

Humility is not self-hate. Humility is teachability. Listen.

Learning implies change. If we haven't changed, we haven't learned.

We can develop the ability to choose our thoughts and feelings. Then we can master our self. Otherwise, we cannot.

You don't 'find' your passion, your purpose, your vision. You build them through years of work.

Life's Greatest Opportunity

The ability to pursue your passions in life comes only after grinding through the labor of real self-sacrifice.

Virtue's counterfeits can be seen everywhere. Substitutes for virtue are hollow, never touching nor filling the hole within. Substitutes for virtue are addictive because they leave us emptier than at the outset, craving even more and more, and in worse pain than ever.

Good enough is good enough for now, but not good enough for tomorrow.

"Do your best" is vague and meaningless, and therefore a frustrating or useless distraction.

Do not be yourself. Be better than your self.

Life's Greatest Opportunity

Doing only what comes naturally results in dwindling toward the mean.

Children and animals act only according to their nature. But much of our purpose in life is to rise above what is natural in us.

We can produce technologies that far exceed the functionality of each human capability taken in isolation. Yet we cannot produce a package of technologies that begins to approach a broad range of human capabilities performed in whole harmony – playing basketball on a team, and telling a joke, and landscaping a garden, and soothing a troubled heart… Humanity prevails.

Pursuing an MBA straight out of an undergraduate program in business is best suited for those living in fear.

Life's Greatest Opportunity

I dare you to study things with no apparent usefulness just because you take delight in the exploration of curiosity.

The book that you are the least comfortable with is the one that you need to spend the most time with, not the one you already are conformed into.

Read as much as little as often as possible.

Do not read a book completely. All books contain too many words. This too.

In order to do better, or to become better, we must first think better.

Right now, determine to do one thing one bit better today than before. Lead the way!

Life's Greatest Opportunity

Nobody's perfect. True, but... we must be striving to be better and better each day. Either move forward or fall behind. Everyone can improve somehow.

Success does not require us to run faster than we are capable of. But it absolutely does require us to diligently expand our capabilities.

Present Past Future! When we do something clearly, regretfully wrong – absorb the moment, think back, but mostly, look forward with care.

You are useful, not in spite of your imperfections, but because of them. A flawed person who owns up to their imperfections can touch many.

If people disrespecting you really bothers you, you've got much bigger problems than that.

Life's Greatest Opportunity

To act and live at a higher level, consider a change of mind and heart. To change your mind and heart, act and live on a higher level.

Peace among people comes as there is peace within heart, mind and spirit.

Master your self and you master the world.

Animals and little children do simply as they feel. Adult humans master their feelings by doing what is right regardless of how they feel.

All of us can be a little stronger, a little kinder, a little wiser, a little harder working, and a lot more useful than we think we can.

Those who are comfortable in their routines are not fulfilling their potential to learn, grow, progress and change.

Life's Greatest Opportunity

Imagine if your doctor, financial advisor, auto mechanic, pilot did just enough to get by in school…

A student cut corners to get through school. Now, you realize (laying face up) they are your surgeon. Beware! Others are counting on you.

Our failures matter only if we resist change.

Right now, picture doing one thing one bit better than yesterday. Commit to that in faith, and focus on it throughout your day.

Science is showing that our choices can shape the nature of our brains, and the way our genes work. We are not destined to be how we were born.

A Great Enemy of success, virtue and happiness: "But that's just the way I am."

Life's Greatest Opportunity

Willpower, Self-discipline, Self-mastery: Think less about denial; it's more about power and liberation.

Q: What can I do about my boyfriend? girlfriend? boss? co-worker? roommate? mother? father? neighbor? A: Nothing. Refine your approach.

If we compare ourselves to others, either... 1. We will become vain, or 2. We will turn bitter. Compare yourself only to your past self.

All your hopes and dreams, all your knowledge and skills, all your character and virtue hinge on your exercising self-mastery.

All books are useless – unless you take a bit from them, and act on it.

Instead of saying, "I wish..." say, "I will..." It's in your hands.

Life's Greatest Opportunity

Do not accept the idea that what you have been (or what you are today) determines what you can become tomorrow. Learn, grow, change.

The obstacle between you and your dreams is your hesitation to adapt or change. It doesn't require a major move all at once, just persistence.

Getting out of your comfort zone is far more important than getting into the "best" school, major, club, job, etc.

Three Prime Things to learn in college: curiosity, self-discipline, other-centeredness. All the rest is ancillary.

Karma, Justice, The Law of The Harvest, or whatever... You are becoming perfectly suited for the life that you are building for yourself.

Life's Greatest Opportunity

Do not dislike change. Your life depends on it.

If you are resisting change, you are resisting life.

Pay no attention to voices requiring you to be perfect. And pay no attention to temptations to slack off.

Never hold yourself to perfection. It will just make you either vain or dejected. Just improve. And obviously, don't expect it of others.

Do Not Seek to comfort yourself with, "But that's very normal." You were born and destined to become better than normal, common, ordinary.

Don't bother getting an education if you already know what you think, or if you are what you want to be. All set and sure? School's not for you.

Life's Greatest Opportunity

Like tending a garden to be much more than it would be if left to nature, so too we must tend ourselves to become above and beyond our nature.

Are you letting your capabilities dictate your dreams? Or are you developing capabilities to fulfill your dreams?

Before you outperform the competition, you must outperform your self.

If someone offers the "secrets" of: success, business, leadership, investing, life – run away laughing. Simple truth is right in front of you.

We can't worry over, complain about, or act on the problems of society and government (or individuals) until we first look into ourselves.

Life's Greatest Opportunity

We can't say we are truly learning if we are not changing. Knowledge may be cheap, but wisdom is hard work.

"Just do your best," unless you are eager to grow.

Be true to yourself, except those parts that need to change.

Follow your passion, unless it blinds you, or unless you have a higher calling than self-serving self-centeredness.

THE SPIRIT WITHIN

There is more to life than meets the eye – far more than physics, chemistry and biology. We are body, mind, heart, and spirit.

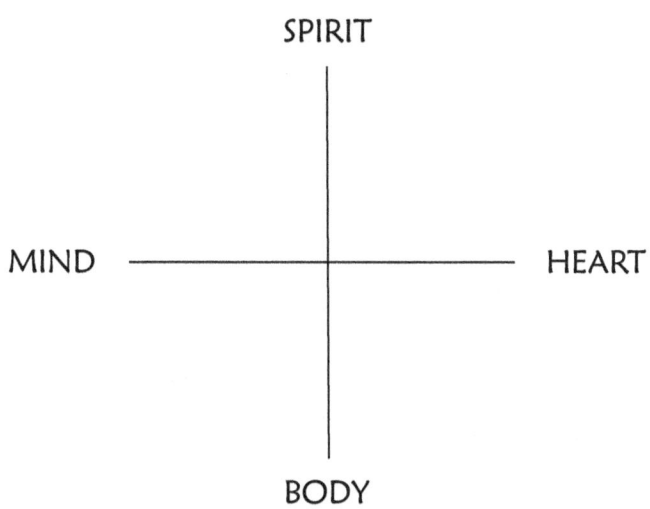

We have four kinds of feelings: physical, mental, emotional, and spiritual. Although connected, they are not equivalent. Learn to discern those differences.

The Spirit Within

Sciences exist so that we can more frequently and longer immerse our selves in the crafts, arts, humanity and spirit at the heart/core of life.

Most Vital Questions: 1) Why am I here? 2) What is my purpose? 3) Am I my brother's keeper? Get these right, and you're on the way.

There is a hunger in all of us to grow and progress, to learn, to change for the better.

Searching for a path with meaning and heart? Feed your curiosity. Follow your desires to help others. Play with creativity.

ONWARD

This work is not complete. It is not finished. This is not the end.

Somebody woke up today to a perfectly normal day, not knowing it would be their last. Appreciate all of it. And be wise.

Tomorrow is a better day.

Get to work.

The Secret to Success
is no secret at all.

It is plainly obvious,
simple and clear.

The only hidden mystery
is whether
we will live it.

www.ingramcontent.com/pod-product-compliance
Lightning Source LLC
Chambersburg PA
CBHW020921180526
45163CB00007B/2825